EARLY INTERMEDIATE LEVEL

CLASSICAL PIANO MASTERS

22 PIECES BY 15 COMPOSERS

ISBN 978-1-5400-8399-9

Visit Hal Leonard Online at
www.halleonard.com

Contact us:
Hal Leonard
7777 West Bluemound Road
Milwaukee, WI 53213
Email: info@halleonard.com

In Europe, contact:
Hal Leonard Europe Limited
42 Wigmore Street
Marylebone, London, W1U 2RN
Email: info@halleonardeurope.com

In Australia, contact:
Hal Leonard Australia Pty. Ltd.
4 Lentara Court
Cheltenham, Victoria, 3192 Australia
Email: info@halleonard.com.au

CONTENTS

MINUET IN G MAJOR
from THE NOTEBOOK FOR ANNA MAGDALENA BACH, Appendix 116

Anonymous

GAVOTTE II: LA MUSETTE

from ENGLISH SUITE NO. 6, BWV 811

JOHANN SEBASTIAN BACH
1685–1750

PRELUDE IN C MAJOR
from THE WELL-TEMPERED CLAVIER, BWV 846

JOHANN SEBASTIAN BACH
1685–1750

THREE PIECES
from FOR CHILDREN, Sz. 42

BÉLA BARTÓK
1881–1945

9

Allegro robusto.

21.

MINUET IN G MAJOR
WoO 10, No. 2

LUDWIG VAN BEETHOVEN
1770–1817

SONATINA NO. 1 IN G MAJOR
Anh. 5, No. 1

LUDWIG VAN BEETHOVEN
1770–1827

Romanza

Allegretto (♩.= 76)

RONDINO

ANTONIO DIABELLI
1781–1858

THE DOLL'S COMPLAINT
Les Plaintes d'une Poupée

CÉSAR FRANCK
1822–1890

SARABANDE
from SUITE IN D MINOR, HWV 437

GEORGE FRIDERIC HANDEL
1685–1759

GERMAN DANCE IN D MAJOR
Hob. IX: 22, No. 2

JOSEPH HAYDN
1732–1809

Allegretto

MINUET IN G MAJOR
K. 1

WOLFGANG AMADEUS MOZART
1756–1791

Minuetto da Capo al Fine

SELECTED SCOTTISH DANCES
from SIX SCOTTISH DANCES, WoO 218

FRIEDRICH KUHLAU
1786–1832

No. 2

No. 3

No. 5

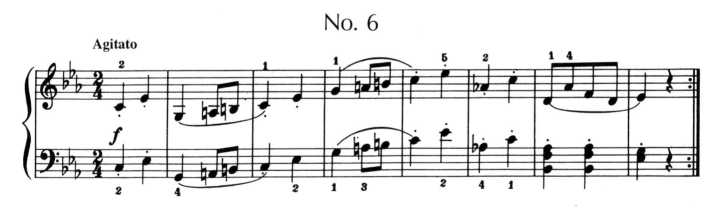

No. 6

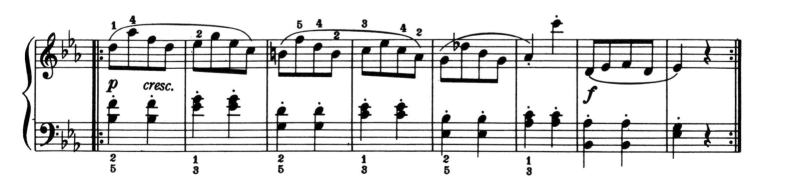

TO A WILD ROSE
from WOODLAND SKETCHES, Op. 51, No. 1

EDWARD MACDOWELL
1860–1908

With simple tenderness (♩ = 88 M.M.)

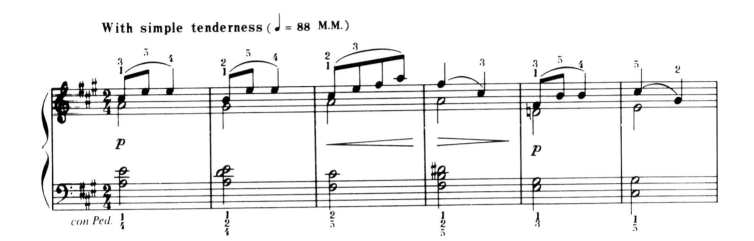

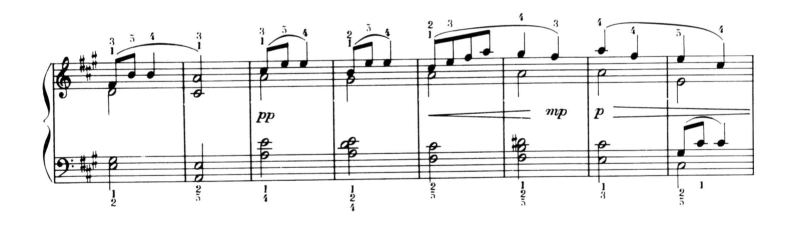

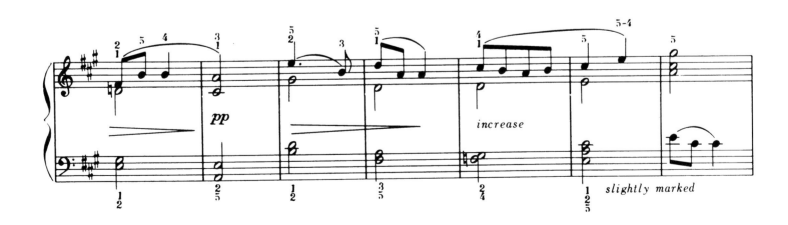

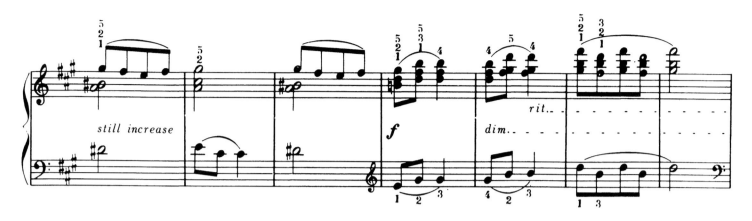

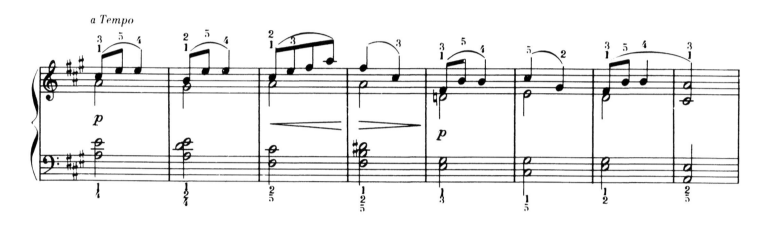

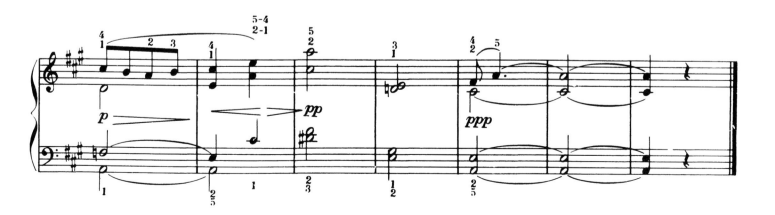

LA TAMBOURIN

JEAN-PHILIPPE RAMEAU
1683–1764

WALTZ IN A MAJOR

FRANZ SCHUBERT
1797–1828

SOLDIERS' MARCH
from ALBUM FOR THE YOUNG, Op. 68, No. 2

ROBERT SCHUMANN
1810–1856

Munter und straff *(gay but strict)*

ITALIAN SONG
from ALBUM FOR THE YOUNG, Op. 39, No. 15

PYOTR IL'YICH TCHAIKOVSKY
1840–1893